Journal

A NEW SEXUAL YOU

_____

For information contact: Slaytor's Playhouse, LLC

Slaytor's Playhouse
ATTN: Vernon Scott
430 Northside Dr E Ste 160
Box #317
Statesboro, GA, 30458

info@slaytorsplayhouse.com
http://www.slaytorsplayhouse.com

ISBN: 978-1-7366319-5-9

Published October 2022

INSTRUCTIONS

It is recommended that users of this journal be as honest as possible in their self-reflection process. There are **10** writing prompts to assist you in your journey of self-discovery and exploration. Because this is your personal journey, there is **no minimum or maximum** to how much you write. There is also no requirement for completing the prompts in order; however, it is recommended.

This journal is also an adult coloring book. Decorate the pages however you wish; this includes the blank pages. Allow your creativity to drive you forward. Create backgrounds. Influence the designs. Bend the preconceived genders into something new. Add a 3D element if you want. Make the images your own.

There are no wrong answers. There are no wrong designs. Do whatever is best for you.

Please use coloring pencils

PROMPT 1

PROMPT 1

Have I consented to myself? If so, what have I consented to, and what does that mean to me? What is preventing me from consenting to myself? Is the lack of consenting to myself preventing me from my goals?

_____

_____

_____

_____

_____

_____

_____

_____

_____

_____

_____

_____

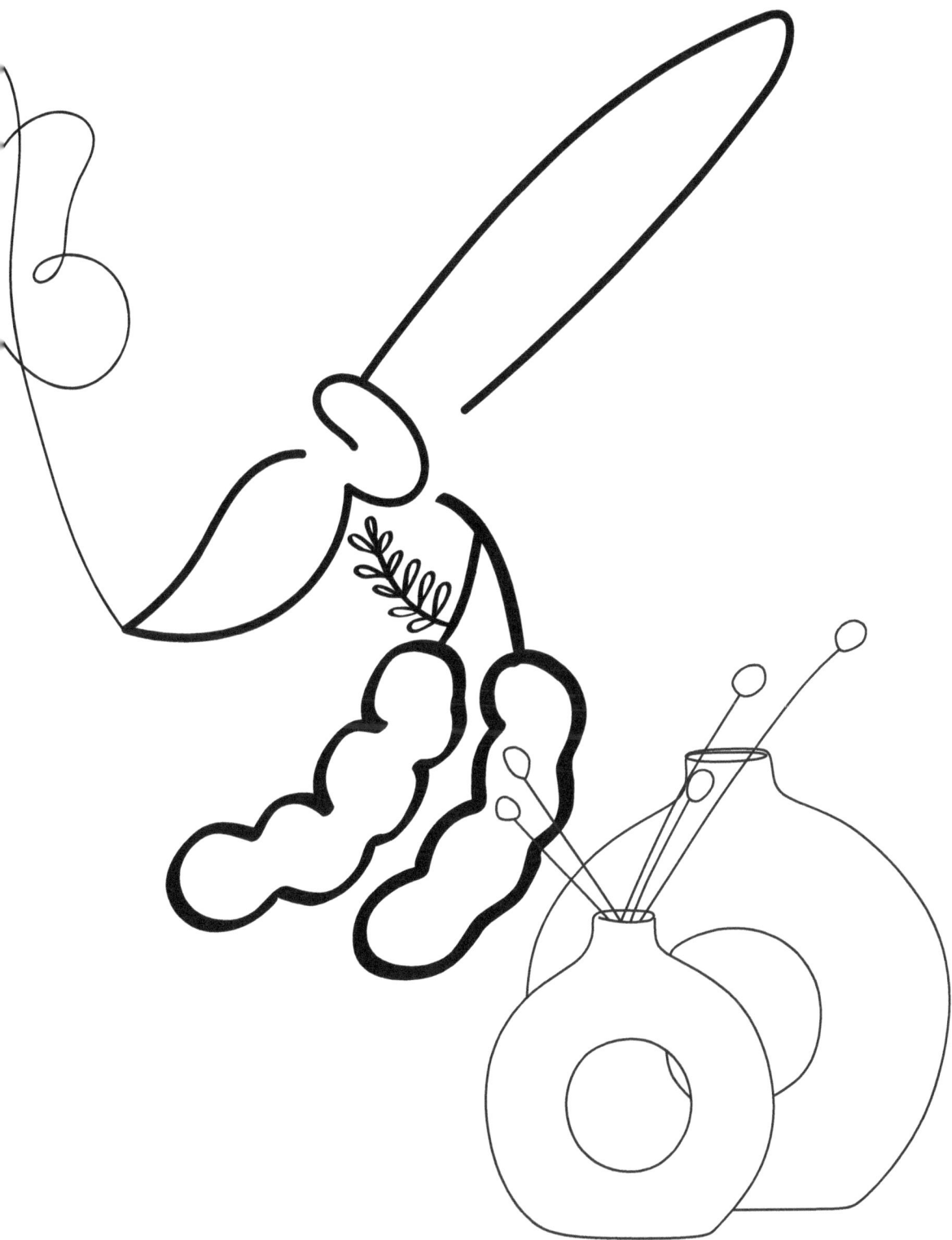

PROMPT 2

PROMPT 2

What does consent mean to me? How does it look and sound? How does consent feel? When am I most comfortable with providing consent?

_____

_____

_____

_____

_____

_____

_____

_____

_____

_____

_____

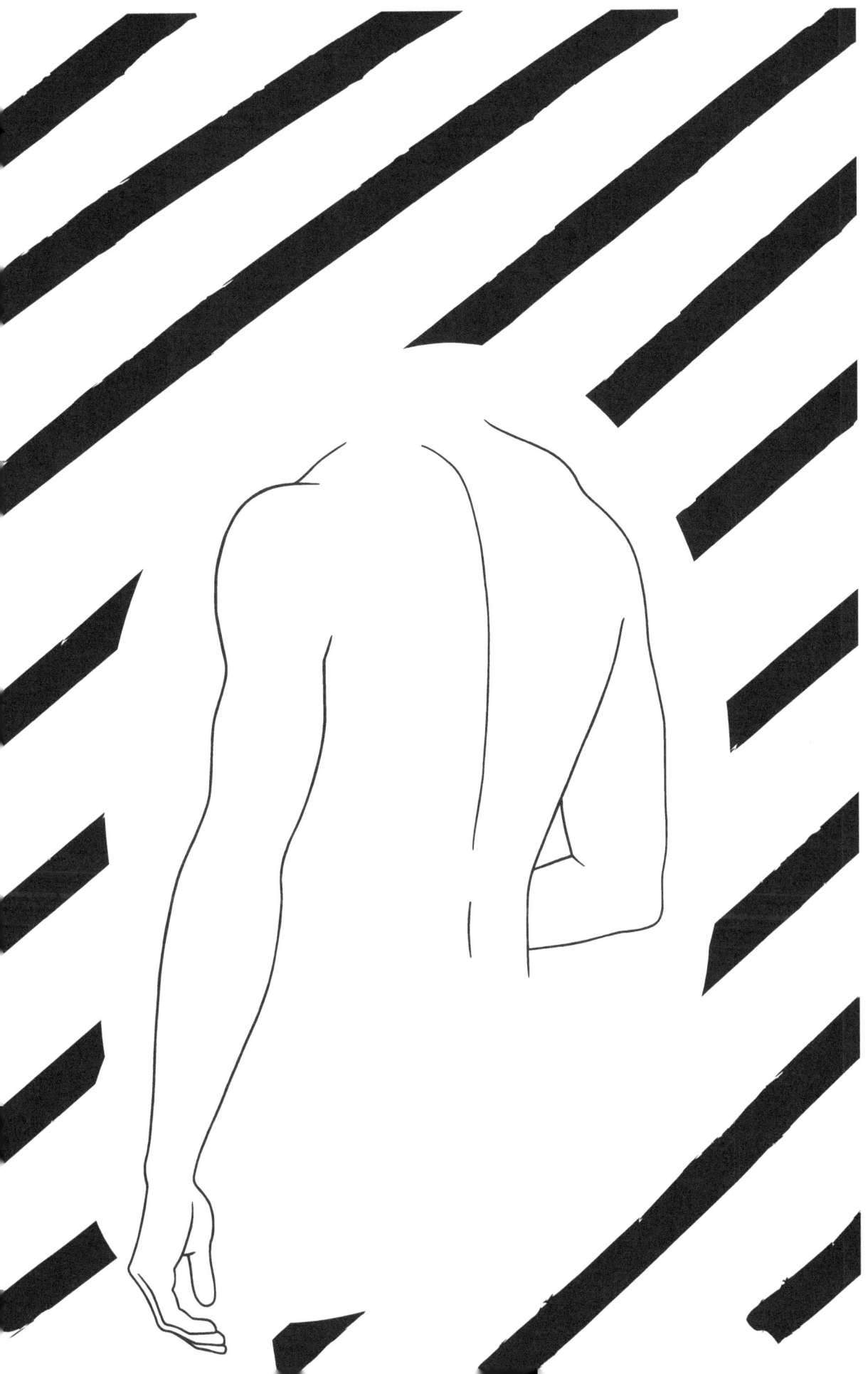

PROMPT 3

PROMPT 3

What prevents me from trusting others? How often am I willing to provide trust to others? How does someone gain my trust? What circumstances allow me to give trust to others?

_____

_____

_____

_____

_____

_____

_____

_____

_____

_____

_____

_____

_____

PROMPT 4

PROMPT 4

What messages have I received over the years related to sexuality? What messages have I received about how I must express my sexuality and sexually perform?

_____

_____

_____

_____

_____

_____

_____

_____

_____

_____

_____

_____

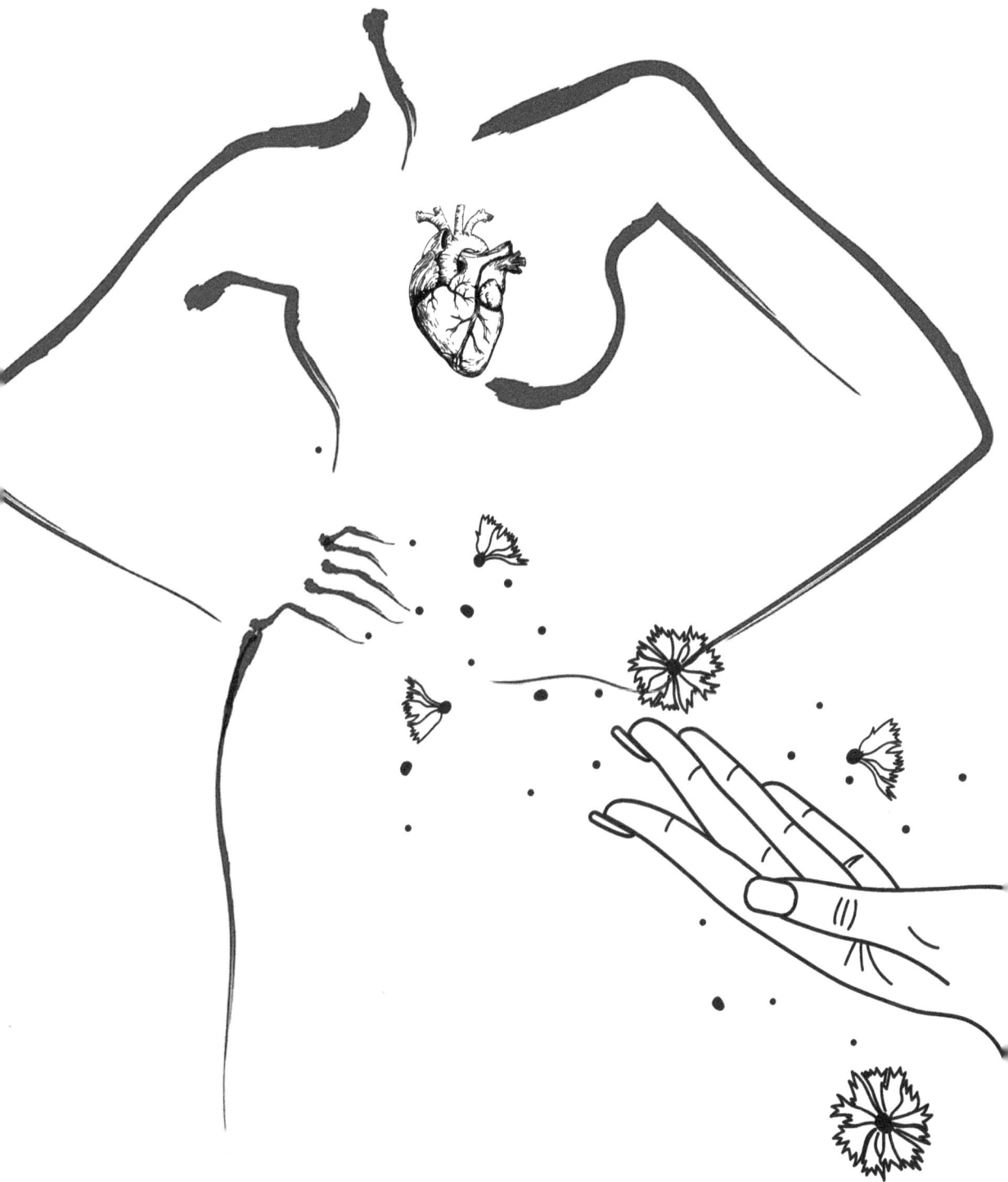

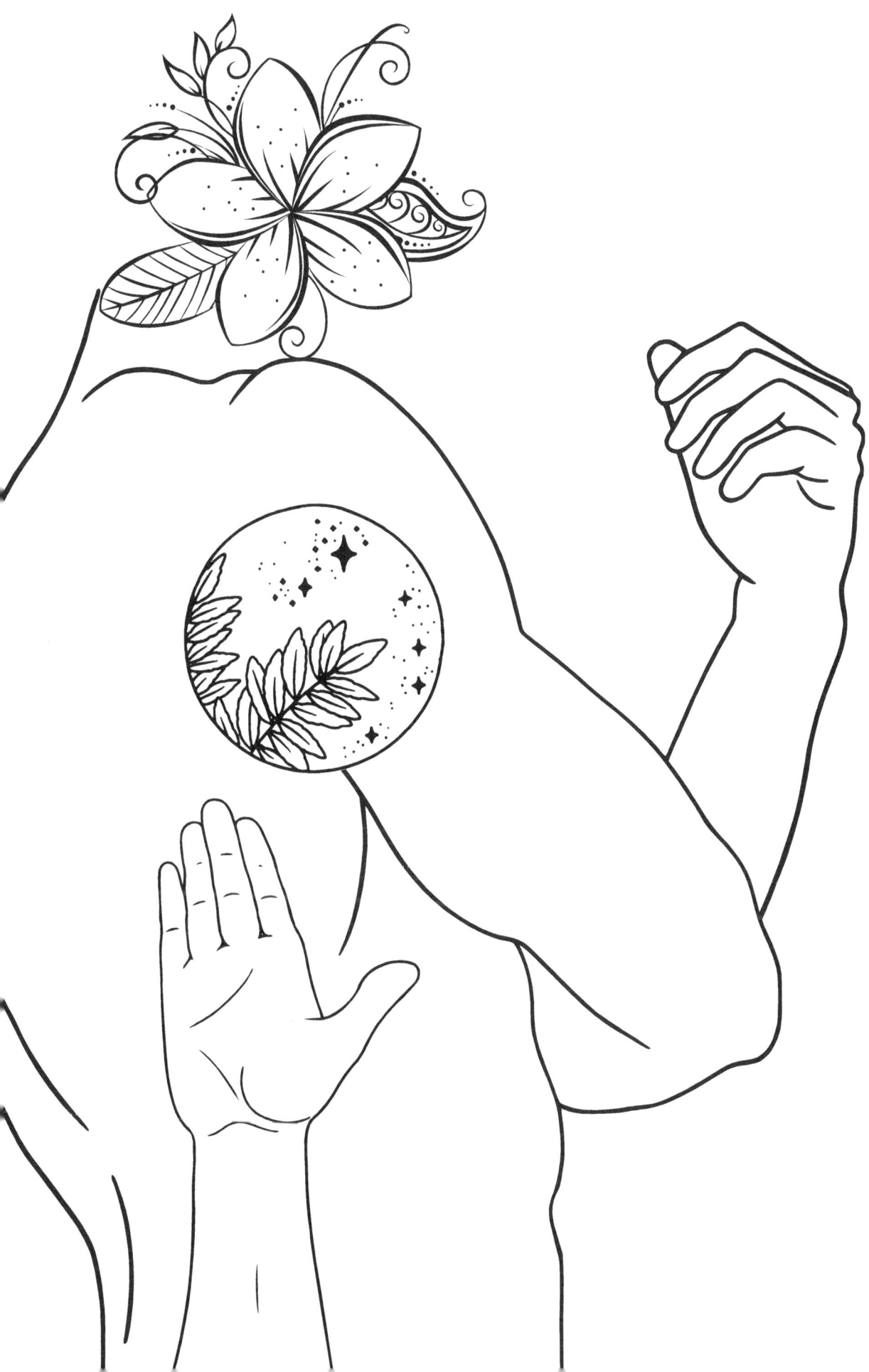

PROMPT 5

PROMPT 5

Do I believe the messages that I received about how I must express myself sexually with myself or a partner? What influences whether or not I believe those messages?

_____

_____

_____

_____

_____

_____

_____

_____

_____

_____

_____

_____

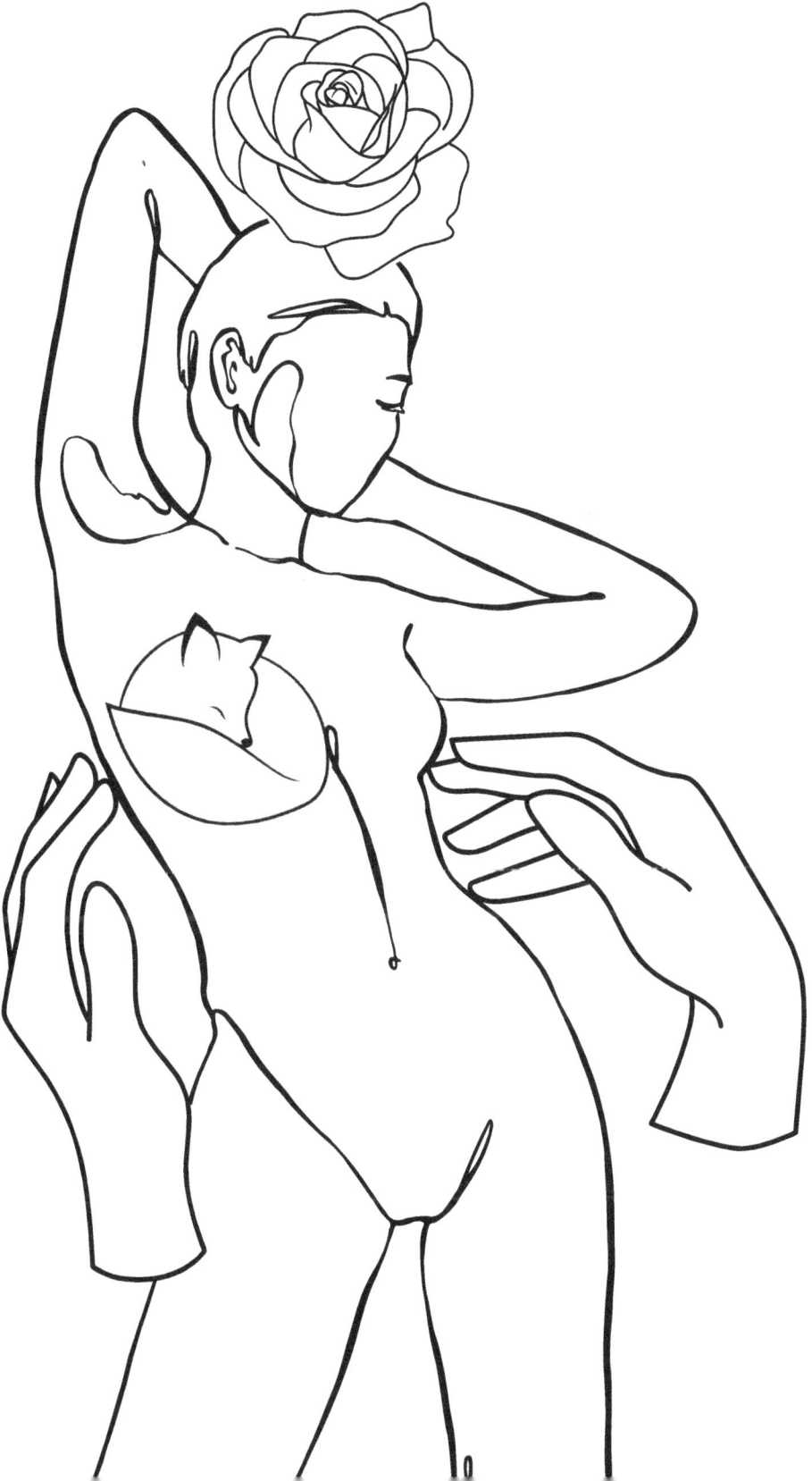

PROMPT 6

PROMPT 6

If I were to express my sexuality in a way that opposed the messages I received over the years, would I feel supported in my decisions? What does that support look like for me?

_____

_____

_____

_____

_____

_____

_____

_____

_____

_____

_____

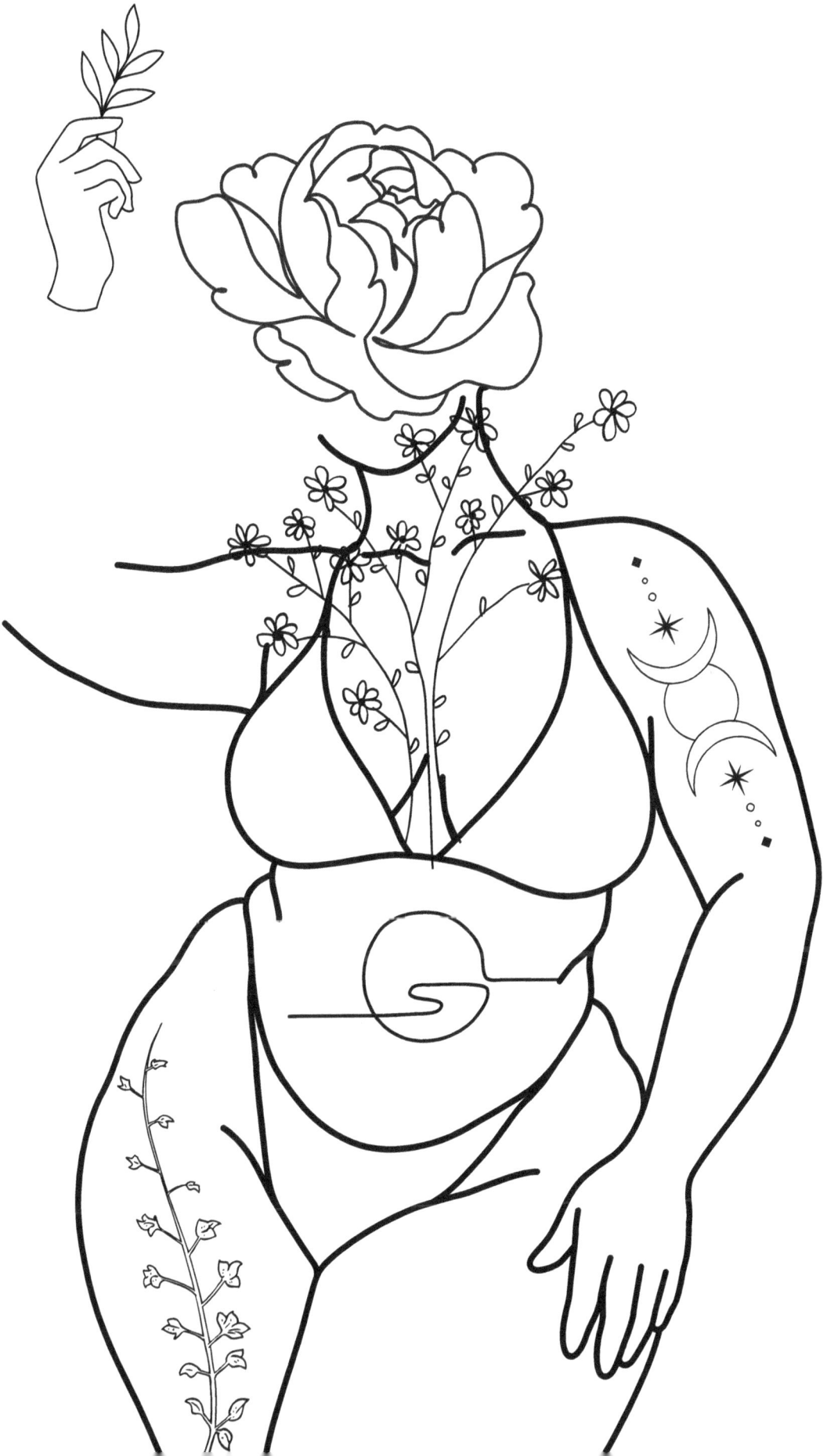

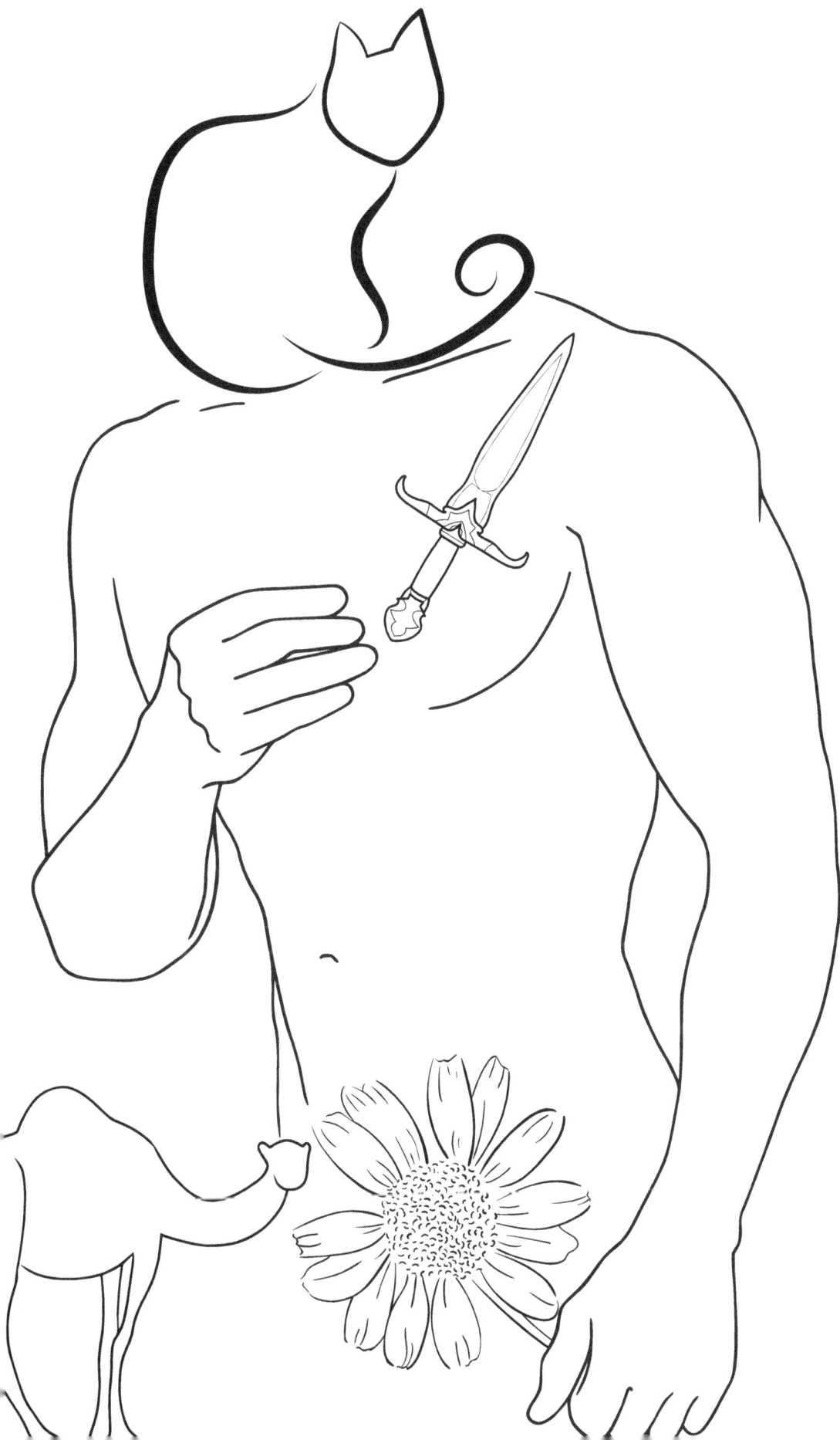

PROMPT 7

PROMPT 7

If I could write a new message regarding sexuality and how it is expressed, what would the message say? If there was no judgment, fear, or shame related to sex, how would I choose to express my sexuality?

_____

_____

_____

_____

_____

_____

_____

_____

_____

_____

_____

_____

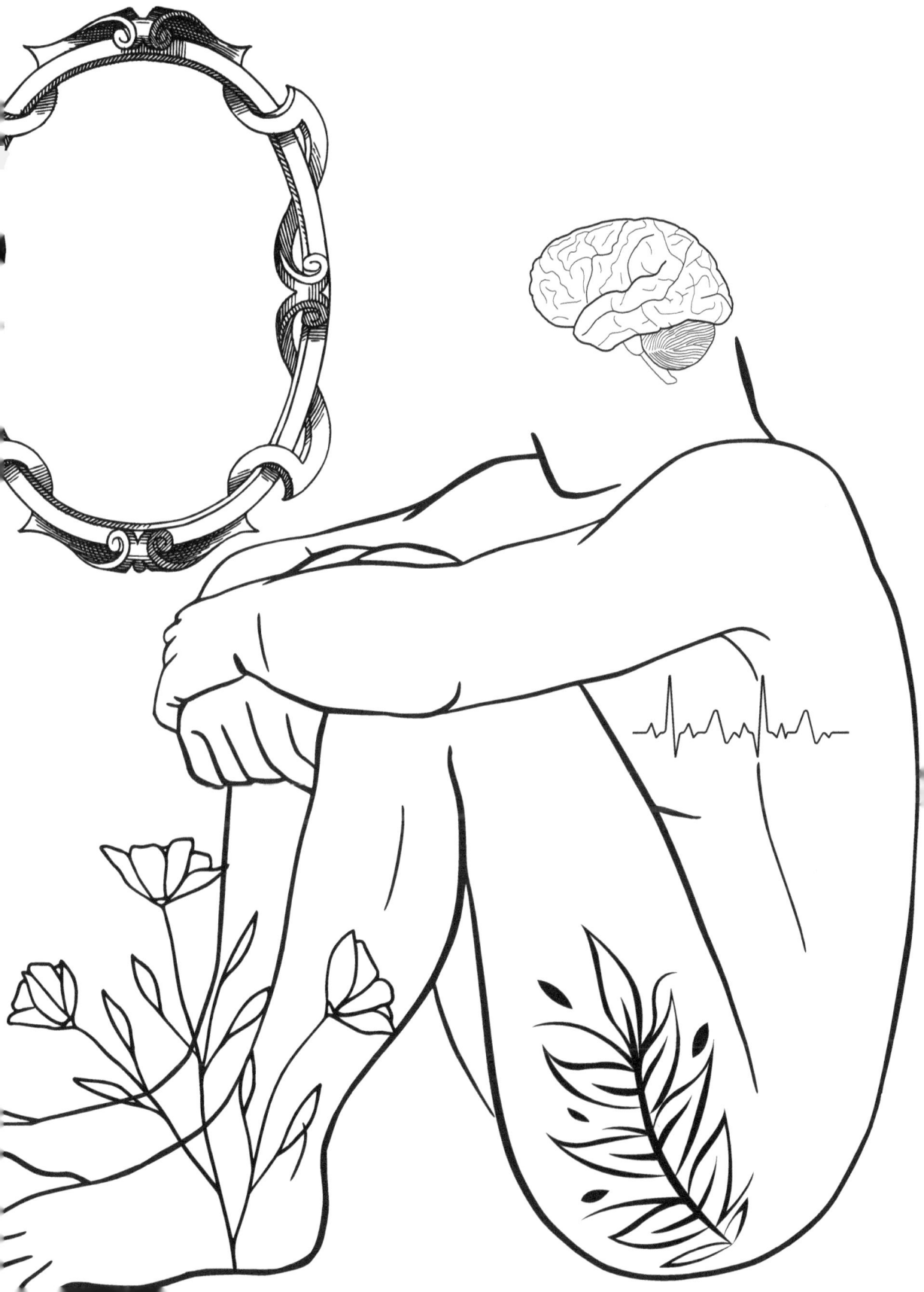

PROMPT 8

PROMPT 8

What do I want/desire from my sexual experiences? What do I want/desire from myself during a sexual experience with others? What do I want/desire from myself during a sexual experience with myself?

_____

_____

_____

_____

_____

_____

_____

_____

_____

_____

_____

_____

_____

PROMPT 9

PROMPT 9

What do I need from my sexual experiences? What do I need from myself during a sexual experience with others? What do I need from myself during a sexual experience with myself?

_____

_____

_____

_____

_____

_____

_____

_____

_____

_____

_____

_____

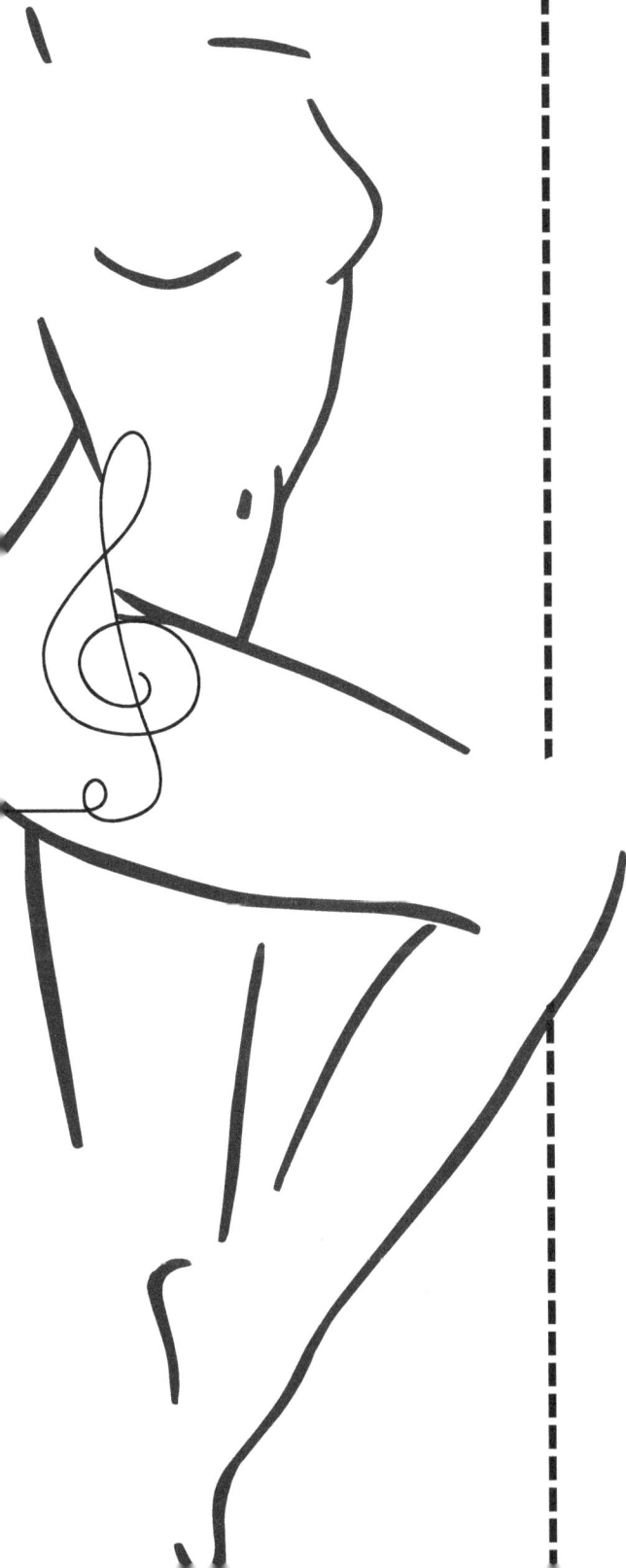

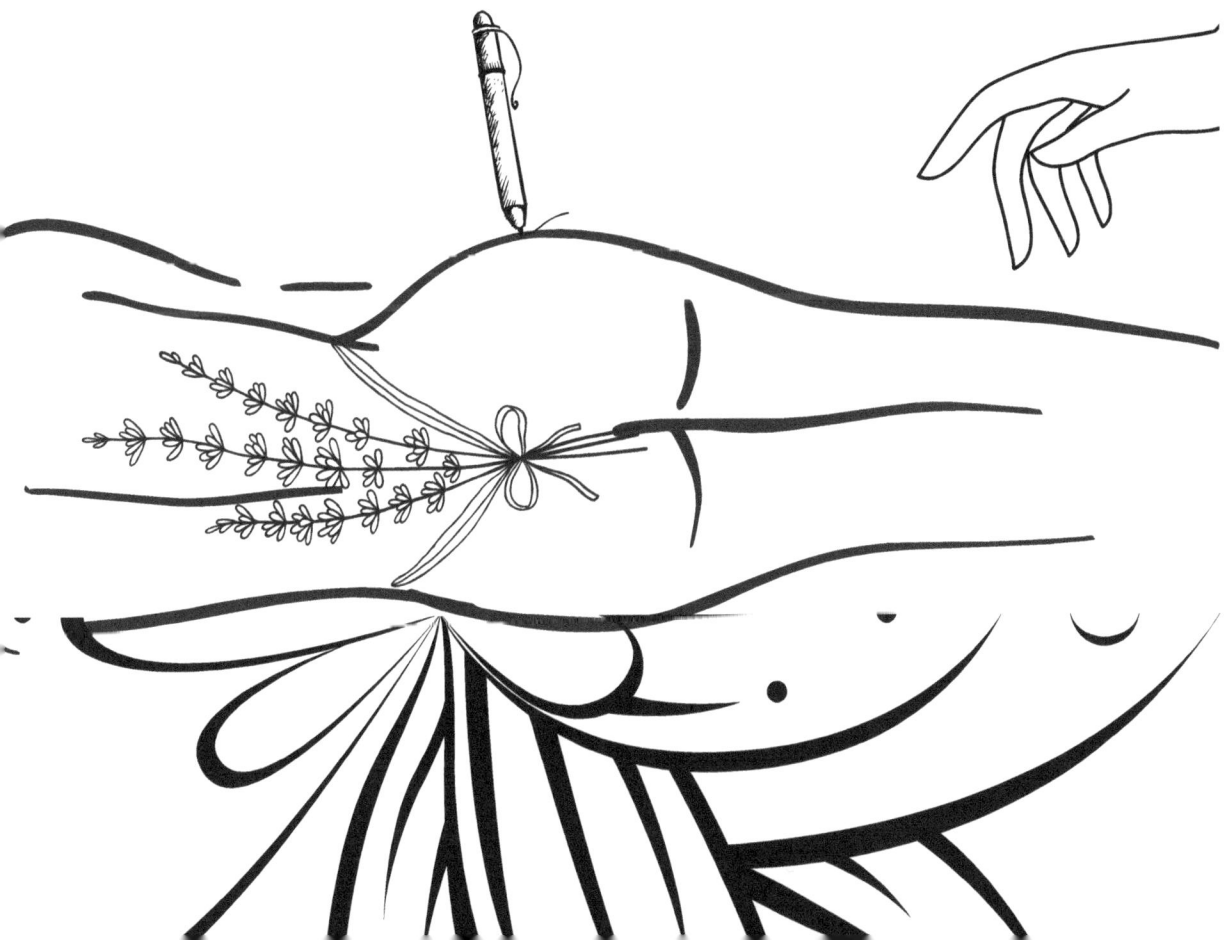

PROMPT 10

PROMPT 10

Do I masturbate? Are there any messages I received that influence whether or not I masturbate? What does masturbation mean, look like, and sound like to me? Am I comfortable with masturbation?

_____

_____

_____

_____

_____

_____

_____

_____

_____

_____

_____

_____

_____

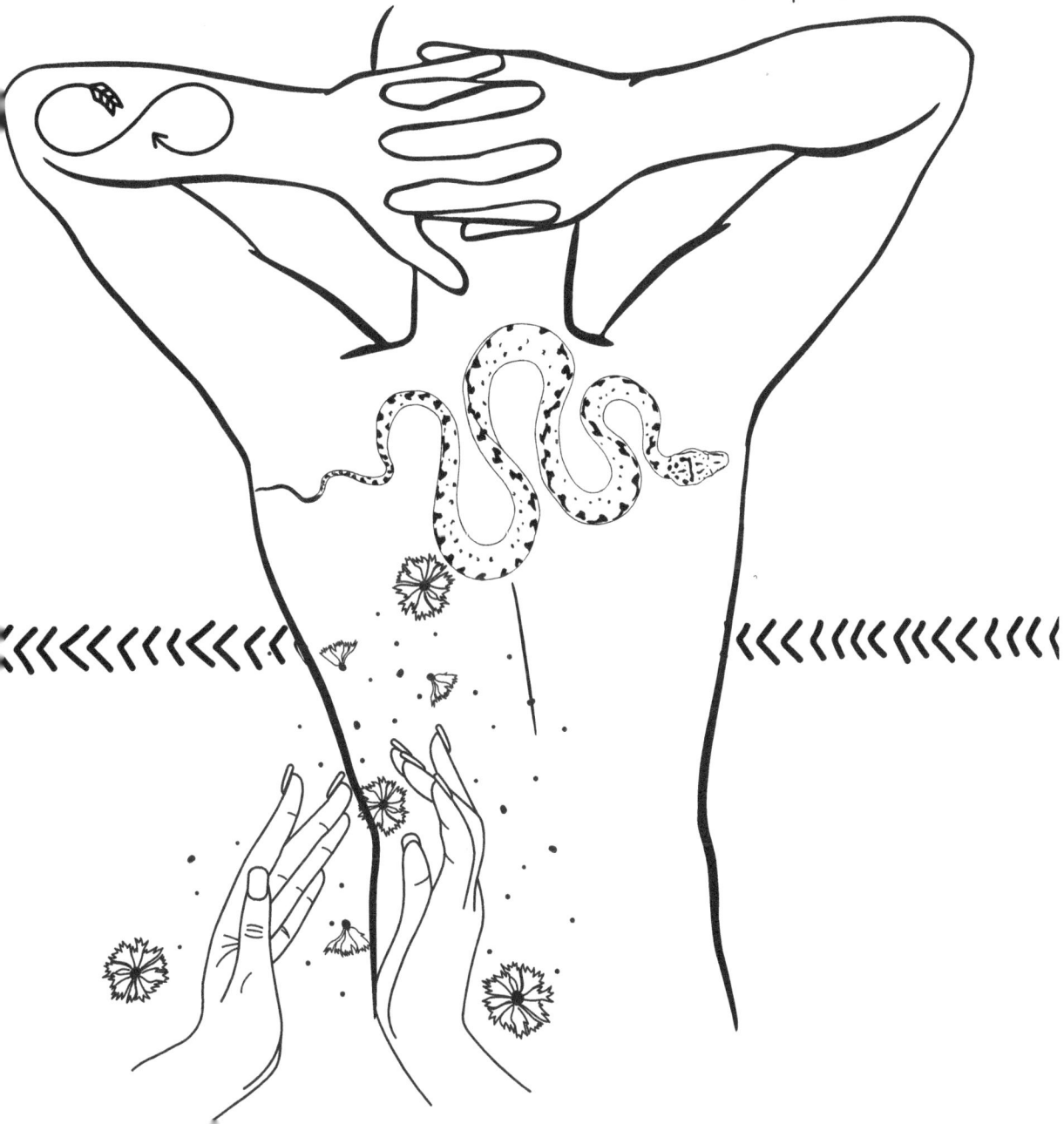

WRITE ON

www.ingramcontent.com/pod-product-compliance
Lightning Source LLC
Chambersburg PA
CBHW080919100426
42812CB00007B/2326